Collectibles

4 –

$\dfrac{1}{19}$

TIFFANY GLASS

TIFFANY GLASS

CHARTWELL
BOOKS, INC.

Published by Chartwell Books
A Division of Book Sales Inc.
114 Northfield Avenue
Edison, New Jersey 08837
USA

0-7858-0989-9

This book is produced by
Quantum Books Ltd
6 Blundell Street
London N7 9BH

Project Manager: Rebecca Kingsley
Project Editor: Judith Millidge
Designer: Wayne Humphries
Editor: Clare Haworth-Maden

The material in this publication previously appeared in
The Art of Louis Comfort Tiffany, The Art of Tiffany

QUMTFG
Set in Times
Reproduced in Singapore by United Graphic Ltd
Printed in Singapore by Star Standard Industries (Pte) Ltd

CONTENTS

LOUIS COMFORT TIFFANY'S EARLY INFLUENCES

Tiffany is a name that has become part of American legend. Today it conveys several different things, but there is a certain vagueness about the people behind the name. First, there is Tiffany, the founder of the New York jewelry and silver store, the smartest place to buy diamonds, which was immortalized by Truman Capote in his novel and Audrey Hepburn in the movie *Breakfast at Tiffany's*. Then there is Tiffany the artist, the foremost American exponent of Art Nouveau, creator of the beautiful Tiffany lamps and Favrile glass vases that achieve fantastically high prices in today's salerooms.

There was a famous father, Charles Lewis Tiffany, and a famous son, Louis Comfort Tiffany. The man who started it all, Charles Lewis Tiffany, was born in Connecticut in 1812, the son of a prosperous textile-maker. He gained business experience at an early age, working in his father's textile mill, managing his general store in Connecticut and occasionally making buying trips to New York City. In 1837, when he was 25, he borrowed $1000 from his father and invested in a small stationery and fancy-goods store with a partner, John B. Young. The store that was to become the internationally famous jewelry emporium began life as Tiffany and Young (it became Tiffany & Co. when John Young retired) on Broadway, opposite City Hall Park.

TIFFANY & CO.
The times were not prosperous and receipts on the first day totaled only $4.98. But the business went rapidly from strength to strength. Charles Tiffany was a man born to sell. He courted a mass market with "Useful and Fancy Articles," bronze statuettes, Japanese lacquer-

Left: The famous wistaria lamp, with its bronze tree-trunk base and irregular lower border designed by Mrs. Curtis Freshell of Tiffany Studios. Over a thousand pieces of colored glass are skillfully worked into the shade.

Opposite page: Louis Comfort Tiffany was the son of Charles Lewis Tiffany, the founder of one of the United States' most exclusive stores, Tiffany & Co. Instead of following in the footsteps of his father, Louis chose to become an artist.

Right: A page from a catalog of jewelry designed by Tiffany & Co,. New York, c. 1890. By then the store was famous, a symbol of democratic luxury that everyone aspired to visit.

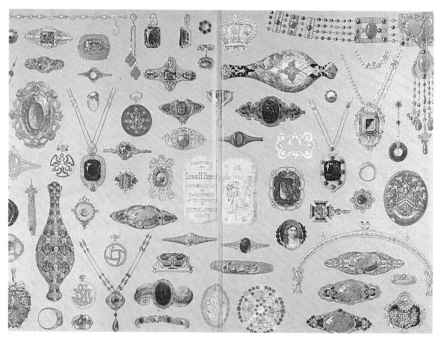

Below: Tiffany & Co.'s premises in New York. Originally located on Broadway, the emporium now stands on Fifth Avenue.

ware, cutlery, toiletries, Tiffany Timer stop-watches, Chinese umbrellas, fans, and curiosities, Venetian-glass writing implements, "seegar" boxes, and Native American artifacts. He had a gift for anticipating popular taste and recognized the appeal of novelty.

THE "KING OF DIAMONDS"

At first gems were promoted only as "best-quality imitation jewelry," but by 1841 Tiffany and Young were buying the real thing in Europe, proudly describing themselves as the only store in New York with a representative abroad: John Young. He was in Paris in 1848 when revolution broke out against King Louis Philippe. The price of diamonds dropped by half and Charles Tiffany was ready to buy. Two years later, Tiffany's opened a Paris branch. It bought diamonds from the fabulous collection of the Hungarian Prince Esterhazy and acquired Marie Antoinette's girdle of diamonds. Later, when the Empire fell, Tiffany's would buy the French crown jewels. Many of the European monarchies were shaky and Tiffany's acted as a middleman, buying from kings and queens and selling to millionaires.

With his financial strength and his ability to make a quick decision, Charles Tiffany could take advantage of bargains and opportunities whenever they occurred. For example, in 1877 the Tiffany Diamond was found in South Africa. It weighed 128.51 carats and Tiffany purchased it for $18,000. He became known as the "king of diamonds," catering for the crowned heads of Europe, selling to the new American industrial barons and millionaire families and advising presidents from the time of Abraham Lincoln.

As well as displaying the million-dollar Tiffany Diamond and providing for the extravagant tastes of the extravagantly wealthy American families, Charles Tiffany set out to cater for the popular market. And he was a shrewd entrepreneur. In the firm's early days he prowled around the New York docks, bargaining with sea captains and snapping up exotic imports from the Orient. Although Tiffany's became the preeminent New York jeweler and silversmith for the next hundred and fifty years, it never became a store for the super-rich alone. Its democratic attitude of treating every customer equally made it a very American symbol of luxury, something everyone could aspire to. Charles Tiffany acquired a reputation for high standards of quality, for foresight and integrity. No haggling or discounts were allowed, even for presidents.

TIFFANY'S STOCK

Items for the average income were always stocked, novelties and curios from the Far East were imported. Charles Tiffany was one of the first to look beyond Europe, and Japanese arts in particular caught the American imagination. Tiffany & Co. had a great influence on the development of silversmithing in the United States, promoting quality and design to match Europe and encouraging and commissioning American craftsmen. From the start, the store sponsored American craftsmanship and established Tiffany silverware by hiring the best-known silversmith in New York, John Moore, to work exclusively for it.

When John Moore retired, his son, Edward Moore, succeeded him and bought the store international fame for its silver for over 40 years. His elegant silver tea set won a prize

Above: A necklace of diamonds and enamelled gilt by Tiffany & Co., New York, 1870. From producing "best-quality imitation jewelry," Charles Tiffany became a "king of diamonds."

at the 1867 Paris Exposition, the first time an American silver company had been honored by a foreign jury. In the 1878 Exposition he won the Gold Medal. European silver houses bought his pieces as patterns for their own ware. The Tiffany silver workshops grew from employing a mere handful of artisans to 500, and new mechanized processes were adopted. Edward Moore played a very influential role among the artists and craftsmen of New York, for he not only set new standards for *objets d'art* in America, but was also a man of great knowledge and sophisticated appreciation. Indeed, Tiffany's brought a kind of civilizing zeal to retailing, taking it upon itself to improve manners and style along with design. Moore's work, and his fine collection of Oriental and antique glass, had a great influence on the artistic development of the young Louis Comfort Tiffany.

Louis Comfort Tiffany was born in 1848 with a golden spoon in his mouth, as he said himself in *The Artwork of Louis Comfort Tiffany*. He was brought up in an environment where beautiful things were appreciated, where arts and crafts and commerce mingled. He grew up surrounded by rare and beautiful things, learning from them throughout his formative years. He realized the great advantage this gave him and in later life sought to give others a similar esthetic experience in their homes.

LOUIS'S CHILDHOOD

As the eldest son, Louis was intended to continue the family tradition, taking over the flourishing firm of Tiffany & Co. in due course.

Right: A stone-set silver vase, a showpiece designed for the Paris Exposition of 1900 by Tiffany & Co., New York. Charles Tiffany and his silversmith Edward Moore set new standards of quality and design and won many awards.

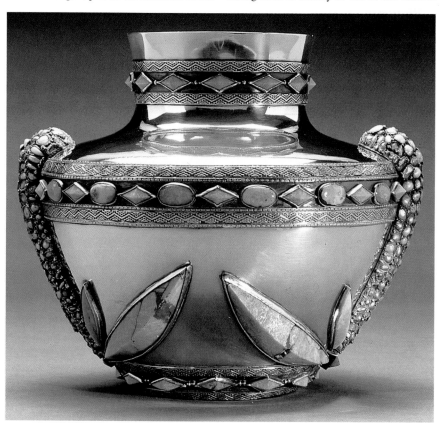

Left: An iridescent glass vase mounted on a silver stand, 1897. The glass was created by Louis Tiffany, and the stand was crafted by Tiffany & Co.'s silversmiths.

Above: This gold vase, with its rich, iridescent sheen, is silky to the touch, thus providing tactile as well as visual pleasure.

From early on, however, it became clear that Louis's nature was unpredictable and mercurial, with great energy, ingenuity, and bursts of creative talent when he was interested in something, coupled with capricious moods and a disruptive wilfullness. He showed little interest in school work when he was sent to boarding school, and then to a military academy. There his interests are recorded as wandering the beach collecting bits of colored glass and pebbles that had been worn into curious shapes by the sea.

ARTISTIC DECISIONS

It was the time of the Civil War. Tiffany & Co. supplied swords, epaulettes and other military paraphernalia. The state of Ohio alone ordered 20,000 cap badges, and Charles Tiffany amassed a fortune. Louis Tiffany left school as the Civil War ended in 1866 with no ambitions for military glory or for commerce. He declared that he wanted to be an artist. Charles Tiffany seems to have accepted his son's rebellious nature and allowed him to choose his own path. Louis Tiffany, while rejecting the commercial life and seeking his own way to fame, came in due course to appreciate the strengths of his father's empire, his knowledge, and his contacts, and the family bond always remained strong.

Typically, he began his career as an artist by joining a painter at work, not by attending classes. George Inness was working in the style of the Barbizon school of French painters, which was beginning to bring a new sense of the landscape into its paintings with light, shadow, and movement, and Inness introduced a kind of unprettified realism to American painting that was vivid and atmospheric. At Inness's studios there were gatherings of young men with wide-ranging interests. There Tiffany met James Steel MacKaye, the playwright who later introduced him to the Aesthetic movement, begun by the painter James McNeill Whistler, with Oscar Wilde as its most flamboyant exponent. This was the beginning of a new movement which refused to accept the cult of the past and wanted to break free of academic traditions, and the movement was taking shape all over Europe.

THE AESTHETIC MOVEMENT

Louis Tiffany found many of his half-formed ideas developed in this way. He responded to the Arts and Crafts movement's dedication to craftsmanship and the turning to nature for inspiration. He was in sympathy with many of the beliefs of the Aesthetic movement. Oscar Wilde talked of bringing artist and craftsman together, bringing art into everyday life, bringing color into the home. Tiffany was to work toward those aims throughout his life.

THE TRIP TO EUROPE

These were exciting times to be an artist. In the following year, 1867, the 19-year-old exhibited a painting at the National Academy of Design and in 1868 he set off for Paris. His trip was in part like the Grand Tour, in part a business trip making contact with his father's European connections (Tiffany & Co. now had branches in Paris, London, and a watchmaking factory in Geneva), but above all learning as an art student. He worked in Paris with the artist Léon Bailly, who had traveled widely in North Africa and Palestine, and had exhibited paintings of Islamic landscapes. He opened the door for Tiffany to enter into another culture, another world of pattern and color.

Tiffany already had an appreciation of

Oriental arts and a knowledge of the exotic Eastern crafts. He responded at once to this new stimulus. The Middle Eastern styles that were to be such a notable feature of Tiffany's exotic interior designs had their birthplace here and were greatly influenced by the Moorish decorations of Spain. Traveling to Spain, he met Samuel Colman, an American artist also traveling and studying, who became a close friend and business associate. Colman was a watercolorist, and from him Tiffany first learned to work in the watercolor medium, preserving his immediate impressions by form

Above: Jack-in-the-pulpit vases were a very popular design. The spectacular, petaled shape of the flower on a slender stem showed off Tiffany's iridescent glass in many colors and combinations.

Left: The rose-bower lamp consists of a leaded glass shade patterned in cabbage roses, with a sculptured bronze base, and was made in 1900.

and color. While Colman's interest was aroused particularly by Islamic textiles, Tiffany was excited by the architecture, and his love of detail begins to emerge in his paintings from this time.

TIFFANY'S VOYAGE OF EXPLORATION
With no anxieties about finances or future security, Tiffany was able to travel freely for a couple of years in Europe, the Middle East, and North Africa. These visits made a strong impression on him and on his creative development. Visiting London at that time, Tiffany found the Aesthetic movement in full swing.

Then, and on later visits, he would have seen the progress of Whistler's Peacock Room, created between 1867 and 1877 for a house in Princes Gate, which had such a crucial influence on the development of interior design – and on Tiffany's style.

ART NOUVEAU
Out of the Arts and Crafts movement and the Aesthetic movement a trend that was later to become of even greater importance in Tiffany's career was about to emerge, developing first of all in France. The term "Art Nouveau" was first coined by Octave Maus and Edmond

Above: On the Way between Old and New Cairo, Citadel Mosque of Mohammed Ali and the Tombs of the Mamelukes. *Oil on canvas, painted by Louis Tiffany c. 1872 following his travels in North Africa and already showing his strength as a colorist.*

Above: The peacock-feather vase. Peacocks were a recurring theme in Art Nouveau, and this vase is a remarkable achievement, giving the impression of pliable fronds of feathers in gleaming, iridescent glass.

Right: Roman and Syrian blown glass of the first century A.D. was being unearthed by archeologists when Louis Tiffany visited Europe, and he would later attempt to replicate its soft and pearly sheen, with considerable success.

Picard in 1881. At first it was applied to the work of painters who were rejecting the old academic traditions and producing their own revolutionary style. Later the term was extended to architecture and art objects. Different countries would, by the end of the century, produce their own versions: in England there was the Liberty style (named after Arthur Liberty's shop, which opened in 1875); in America Tiffany would reign supreme. With strong antiacademic feelings, and a rejection of slavish devotion to the classical tradition and its straight lines, went a new observation and imitation of nature, with lines curved and colors cleared and brightened boldly.

THE FASCINATION OF GLASS

Tiffany had the opportunity on his travels of seeing the great stained-glass windows in the medieval cathedrals of Europe, and his admiration for these was heightened by his fascination with glass as a medium. Antiquity held the beginnings of glass. He was deeply impressed by the qualities of the Roman and Syrian glass of the first century A.D. which was being unearthed by archeologists at the time. Many of the glass objects, buried for centuries, had been affected by metallic oxides in the soil, and these had given the glass surfaces a pearly, iridescent sheen. Each object was complete in itself, without etching or painting, and that appealed to Tiffany strongly.

THE GLASSWORKERS' ART

The art of working in colored glass had been known for centuries. The glowing, jewel-bright,

Left: This double-gourd vase was made in the 1890s. Inspiration for the shape was drawn from antiquity, but the design of contour lines is essentially Art Nouveau.

stained-glass windows of the cathedrals were evidence enough. The high point of the craft was in the fourteenth century, and there had been a decline since the Renaissance. Now the glassworkers' art was lost. It was time to go back to the beginning, to learn the art anew, and already in England Tiffany may have seen the work of William Morris and Company. Burne-Jones designed windows for Morris from 1861, designs which were made up of a number of small pieces of glass of various colors, etching into the glass with metal oxides.

Tiffany had traveled to widen his experience as a painter, but he learned so much more that it fired his creative work throughout his career.

Right: The zinnia lamp. Colorful lamps like this one, with its inspiration of flowers, achieved Tiffany's aim of bringing beauty into the home.

FROM INTERIOR DESIGN TO THE TIFFANY GLASS COMPANY

On his return to America from Europe, Louis Comfort Tiffany first concentrated on his work as a painter, and in 1870 became the youngest member ever to be elected to the Century Club. The following year he became an associate member of the National Academy of Design, and in 1880 a full member of the academy. Tiffany was working at that time in a rented studio at the Y.M.C.A., which was well placed across the road from the National Academy of Design, and he was part of a group of artists which included George Inness, John La Farge, and Samuel Colman.

Preceding page: Duane Street, New York, *painted by Louis Tiffany in 1875, showed his bold originality in its contemporary realism, anticipating the American Ashcan school of painting.*

Below: The luxurious interiors designed by Tiffany had every detail harmonized to a theme. The Islamic style was emphasized with rugs, arches, friezes, and lamps.

His paintings are interesting, in view of his later career, for their strength of color. He believed that line and form were of secondary importance – they disappeared at a short distance, while color remained visible for much longer. He began to use painting techniques closer to those of the Impressionists. He was determined to break away from the dim browns and turgid tones of the past; leaves in his paintings were realistically green, and flesh tones were so fleshy that they provoked acrimonious comment from the critics on his audacity. He drew inspiration from nature, but not as a slavish copyist. His obsession with color and decoration found expression in his Oriental works, in which he showed the influence of his travels and his teachers; in his urban studies he showed his bold originality. He was well ahead of his time when he painted *Duane Street, New York*, anticipating the American Ashcan school in aiming to found an American style based on a realistic portrayal of the contemporary scene. It was because he felt constricted by the narrow views of the National Academy that Tiffany became a founder member of the Society of American Artists, which had a broader view of art.

THE APPLIED ARTS

Tiffany continued to paint all through his career, but it was becoming clear that painting was not enough to express his great creative force. Perhaps, too, as a perfectionist, Tiffany was aware that his painting was not of the highest order – good, but not good enough to satisfy him. Many influences in his life came together to direct him to the wider fields of applied arts. In 1876 a turning point was the Philadelphia Centennial Exposition. Tiffany exhibited nine paintings, but what fascinated him most were the examples of

Left: The dining room at 47 East 34th Street designed for Dr. William T. Lusk had a bronze frieze and transoms of amber glass.

applied arts. Here he again saw the developments of the Arts and Crafts movement that he had encountered in England, such as a wallpaper designed by Walter Crane and a beautiful screen of embroidered peacocks from the Royal School of Art Needlework. Candace Wheeler, herself a master of embroidery, was impressed by the idea that this organization provided profitable work for impoverished gentlewomen in England and was determined that the same should be done in America. To this end she formed the Society of Decorative Art in New York, inviting Tiffany to become involved as a lecturer on painting and pottery.

INTERIOR DESIGN

Very soon this was not enough to satisfy Tiffany, but it brought him to an important decision. He told Candace Wheeler: "I have been thinking a great deal about decorative work, and I am going into it as a profession. I believe there is more in it than in painting pictures." He thus formed Louis C. Tiffany and Associated Artists, with Candace Wheeler and Samuel Colman as partners, and in 1879 began a new career as an interior designer, decorating others' homes.

Tiffany was exceptionally well placed to launch the company, since his father's business contacts meant that he had connections with the right market – the wealthy American elite. The company created homes of exotic magnificence for this group of wealthy families, and soon the word spread and there was praise for the harmonized schemes for rooms, the originality of the designs, and the high quality of the workmanship. Tiffany had a vision of rooms rich with color, ornate detail, sumptuous textiles, and glowing glass.

Right: The drawing room in Stuyvesant Square that Tiffany designed for Hamilton Fish features the ornate magnificence that displayed the wealth and status of the American elite.

The style of decoration had its inspiration in Byzantine, Islamic richness and in Whistler's Peacock Room. It appealed to the taste of the first patrons, many of them *nouveau riche*, who felt that in this rich setting, with a wealth of *objets d'art* displayed, they were clearly demonstrating their importance.

During these years Tiffany was developing his personal style. He was often impatient with the restrictions and traditional tastes of his clients; he was startling and original with his brilliant colors, glass tiles and the stained-glass windows that he introduced into interior settings. His taste in interior design was close to the theatrical, its exotic boldness and strong colors contrasting with the quieter taste of Candace Wheeler. It was difficult for Tiffany to be part of a team, but a team was needed to carry out the first, prestigious commissions.

CRITICAL PRAISE

One of the earliest was the design of the drop-curtain – an experiment in new methods of appliqué – at the Madison Square Theater, which was to open in 1880 with a play written by James Steel MacKaye. The curtain was destroyed by fire before the first season ended, but was replaced by an improved copy which was praised by Oscar Wilde when he visited New York.

Little more than a year after the formation of Louis C. Tiffany and Associated Artists, its work was being praised by the critics. "Perhaps the broadest, most original and richest development yet seen in America," one prestigious magazine on interior design noted. The successful businessmen of the day were commissioning lavish buildings for their homes and businesses and Tiffany was one of the first

to understand the link that must be made between architecture and interior design; he also believed that each room should have its own, unique theme.

THE FIRST INTERIORS

The first complete interior was executed for the home of George Kemp on Fifth Avenue, and had an Oriental, interlaced ceiling with hanging lamps and a frieze painted by Tiffany. He lined the fireplace with his own glass tiles and put panels of opalescent glass in the transoms above the doors. One of the earliest commissions for a public building was for the Veterans' Room of the Seventh Regiment Armory. The design expressed the idea of the war veteran with materials and decorations 'undeniably assimilable and matchable with the huge hard, clanging ponderosities of wars

Left: The bold and colorful effect of Tiffany's design can be seen in this hall and staircase, with its detailed lattice work and Islamic friezes.

Right: Louis C. Tiffany and Associated Artists' design for the Veterans' Room of the Seventh Regiment Armoury.

Below: The sumptious drawing room designed for Mark Twain's mansion in Connecticut pleased the writer immensely.

and tramping regiments." There were ponderous soffit beams, with ax-cuts showing on them, metallic lusters, iron decorations, a large fireplace framed by Tiffany with glass tiles and, over the mantel, framed in hammered iron, was a plaque representing a struggle between a dragon and an eagle. High oaken wainscoting was surmounted with carving of Japanese inspiration and there were also rectangular, bolted panels, Celtic interlaced ornaments, and wrought-iron chandeliers. The colors were the dark browns of iron, leather and oak, lit by transparent glass mosaics suspended in front of large windows.

NOTABLE COMMISSIONS

Glass tiles and a stained-glass window featured in the redecoration of Mark Twain's home in Hartford, Connecticut, where Tiffany placed a window above the dining-room fireplace at the author's suggestion so that "he could watch the flames leap to reach the falling snowflakes." Stencilled decorations designed after Indian motifs were added to the ceiling and walls, and Tiffany supplied amber, turquoise, and brown tiles in transparent and opalescent glass. When he saw the result, Mark Twain said: "The work is not merely and coldly satisfactory but intensely so."

In 1881 two elaborate and troublesome schemes were undertaken at the same time by Associated Artists. A commission to redecorate the home of Ogden Goelet at 59th Street and Fifth Avenue was completed first. The decoration of the Vanderbilt mansion at 58th Street and Fifth Avenue began with Tiffany's scheme being approved by Cornelius Vanderbilt II with great pleasure, but more than a year and a half later Candace Wheeler was still coping with the difficulties, being put to great trouble and expense with the job,

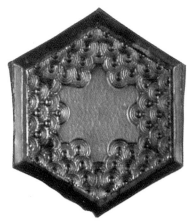

Above: The crowning glory of the East Room in the White House was the floor-to-ceiling glass screen of national emblems in brightly colored panels.

Right: Glass plaques, first produced by Tiffany in the late 1870s while he was carrying out experiments in glass, were incorporated into decorative windows.

and reporting "Mrs. Vanderbilt absolutely refused to have the green plush."

While the Vanderbilt commission was still in progress, Tiffany and Associated Artists' position as the preeminent American decorators was confirmed by an invitation to redecorate rooms in the White House. President Chester Alan Arthur wanted the White House cleaned and renovated before he moved in. He declared that it was like a badly kept barracks. Tiffany certainly changed that with his lavish, ostentatious designs; the work was completed in an astonishing time of seven weeks.

THE WHITE HOUSE

It was said that all Washington was impressed and delighted by the transformation. There was particular praise for Tiffany's glass-mosaic

sconces in the Blue Room, but the crowning achievement of the scheme was the floor-to-ceiling glass screen Tiffany designed, dividing the hallway from the State Dining Room and separating the inner corridor from the public. It was elaborate and exquisite, with brightly colored panels featuring national emblems, eagles, and flags, and was one of the earliest examples of curving free-forms in glass encased in geometric leading.

Recognition as the leading artistic decorators meant that Associated Artists was in great demand. But very soon Tiffany became irritated by the demands of clients – at least in designing the decor for his own rooms on the top floor of the Bella Apartment House at 48 East Street he was able to indulge his own tastes. The problems of matching fabric

shades and swatches furthermore made him impatient, while the development of glass for stained-glass windows and mosaics fascinated and absorbed him.

Tiffany had begun his experiments in glass-making as early as 1872. When he was renting a studio at the Y.M.C.A., he dabbled in experiments, but was persuaded to desist when some kind of explosion occurred. He tried again three years later at Thill's Glasshouse in Brooklyn. He made a close study of medieval stained-glass windows, and then set himself to produce the kind of glass color he wanted. For Tiffany everything began with the glass: pieces of glass were cut to make up the design, then the leading was carefully threaded round the glass. This was a skilled task, requiring time and patience, but the results were true to the artist's designs and turned out to be much superior to the windows and mosaics which started with the outline in lead, the glass then being fixed into the spaces between, made by his competitors.

EXPERIMENTS IN GLASS

Tiffany set up his own glass furnaces in 1878, with a Venetian glass-blower, Andrea Boldoni in charge, and took advantage of the Italian's knowledge of Venetian glass-blowing. Some early Tiffany vases are said to have been clearly influenced by mid-nineteenth-century glass from Murano. This venture was ill-fated: the works burned down twice and Boldoni resigned. But Tiffany continued his experiments at Heidt Glasshouse in Brooklyn, applying for patents for three types of glass in 1880: glass suitable for tiles and mosaics; window glass; and glass with a metallic luster (the earliest mention of what would become the famous Favrile art glass). While Tiffany was making his experiments at Heidt, using the earliest results in glass tiles for mantels and stained glass for windows, John La Farge, the artist and colorist, was also carrying out experiments at the same glasshouse. The two men became rivals, and their rivalry increased over the years as they became fierce competitors for the same commissions. They were both founder members of the American School of Stained Glass.

STAINED-GLASS WINDOWS

One of the most important aims of Tiffany's experiments was to produce glass that would make it possible for the entire design of a window to be carried out by means of the color in the glass itself. This meant that figures, their hands and faces, the folds of draperies, the shadows and lights on landscapes, must all be

Above: This stained-glass window, Hudson River,*was designed for the reception room at the home of Melchior S. Beltzhover at Irvington, New York. The colors achieve an amazing freshness and brillance.*

achieved without using any paint, etching, or enameling. At the Heidt works a new glass was invented by Tiffany with great possibilities and promise. It was given the name "drapery glass" because the sheets of colored glass were styled to represent folds in textiles, with a three-dimensional effect. Workmen moved heavy corrugated rollers over the molten glass, punching and pressing and pulling it about with tongs until the right kind of drape was obtained in varying degrees of translucency

to suit either the right folds of gowns or the voluminous folds of curtains.

"Bull's-eye" effects were produced by whirling the molten glass round on a rod. Solid lumps of glass were pressed into molds while hot, giving a great number of facets; these could be set in windows like brilliant gems, changing color at different angles and catching the light. Tiffany used "bull's-eye" semicircular windows in the Church of the Sacred Heart, New York, in 1876. In effect, the design was

like a series of preserve-jar bottoms. In 1878 he designed a window with St, Mark as the subject for the Episcopal Church in Islip, Long Island, using a series of tangential, circular pieces of glass surrounding the figure, outlined in the broadest way without "drawing" on the glass.

GLASS IN INTERIOR DESIGN

Tiles that were transparent, opaque, marbled, and mottled with swirling streaks of color or gleaming with an iridescent finish were produced. These were used as wall decorations and fireplace surrounds. Opalescent glass was widely used by Tiffany and La Farge in their windows and, as time went on, it became a special characteristic of American stained glass. Tiffany insisted that his stained-glass windows were a purer expression of stained glass than those of medieval glass-makers, because he could dispense with pigment. All the color was in the glass, and it was the way that the light could be varied by the use of opalescent glass and gradations of tone color that enabled him to create special effects. This was the exciting breakthrough.

At the same time as he was absorbed in glass experiments, Tiffany was also continuing to collect Oriental domestic ware, as well as antique glass. This was a new area of collecting at the time, as it was not classical art in the accepted sense. He studied the techniques and designs of everything he collected, for he believed that the best possible process of learning was by close association with beautiful

Left: Luster and Agate tiles featured in many of Tiffany's interior designs. He used them in fireplace surrounds, in decorative friezes around windows and doors, and incorporated them in table tops.

Above: Charles Tiffany commissioned a grand New York residence for his family, with design by Louis Tiffany, who had a studio and apartment on the top stories.

objects, arts, and crafts. He had been in Europe again in 1875, visiting the Paris Exposition. He had traveled with his original mentor, Edward Moore, and was introduced to Samuel Bing, who imported Oriental items and supplied many of the unique objects in Tiffany's collection. For Tiffany, the meeting with Bing was the start of a long friendship and a very auspicious one. Some 20 years later, Bing opened a shop in Paris which he called La Maison de l'Art Nouveau. This gave the movement its focus and official title, and Bing was instrumental in introducing Tiffany's glasswork to Europe.

As Tiffany became increasingly absorbed in his experiments in glass, the team of Associated Artists began to drift apart. In 1883 it was decided to detach the artistic needlework side, controlled by Candace Wheeler.

THE LYCEUM

In the following year his wife, Mary, died of tuberculosis, and the grieving Tiffany turned for solace to the theatrical world, and two friends in particular: Steel MacKaye and Stanford White. MacKaye was contemplating opening a new theater, the Lyceum. Tiffany offered to undertake the work for no fee, just a percentage of the profits, and got the job. It was an exciting project, elevated to the highest level of artistic aims, and it had the benefit of the latest technical advances. It was the first theater to be lit by electric light, and there were new folding seats. Everything in the design, it was said, was a departure from the hackneyed forms of theatrical decoration. The success of the theater design was not matched by that of its first performance, *Dakolar*, which ran for only two months. There were no profits and Tiffany was forced to sue, ending up owning the theater until a new manager was able to put it on a paying basis. In the process he lost money heavily, his excursion into the theatrical world costing him the profits of all his years of hard work in interior design.

THE TIFFANY HOUSE

It was a sad time for Tiffany, and his father felt that the way for Louis to restore himself was to become absorbed again in the artistic world. He announced that he would build a Tiffany family house, and that Louis would be in full charge of its decoration. The Tiffany house was built on Madison Avenue. It was huge, with a massive, arched entrance, a grill and porte-cochère, an elevator, balconies, and loggias. On the top stories Louis Tiffany designed a studio and apartment for himself and his children, and in decorating the studio he produced the first example of American Art Nouveau. The studio appears to have been a glorious, eclectic jungle, richly Indian, with lamps on chains and plants of many lands. It was dominated by a curving, free-form central fireplace, which reached upward in a single column toward the roof. The fireplace was open on four sides so that the light from the blazing logs would illuminate the beautiful things around it.

THE TIFFANY GLASS COMPANY

Tiffany now accepted not only his father's help and advice but also his kind of professionalism. In 1885 he relaunched his business as the Tiffany Glass Company. Set up in a more businesslike way, it catered for professionals rather than private clients, and the glass which later made his name and international fame occupied his attention full-time. He took on the role of creative director and master designer, employed specialist craftsmen and concentrated on his work with a new maturity and

Above: The demand for stained-glass windows by Tiffany increased dramatically from 1887. Windows with floral subjects, such as this trumpet vine leaded window, were popular.

renewed vigor. From this point Tiffany's career began to move strongly ahead into a new phase of success as leading architects gave the Tiffany Glass Company orders for stained-glass windows for homes, churches, and various institutions.

His breakthrough in colored glass for windows coincided with the great religious fervor that was sweeping America. All over the country more and more churches were being built in the new towns growing up along the railroads which crossed from the east coast to the west. In every church, stained-glass windows were in demand. Tiffany inspired the

Above and right: Details from Tiffany's triple-paneled window (designed by Frederick Wilson) for the headquarters of the American Red Cross in Washington, D.C., which was installed in 1918.

fashion, and it was Tiffany windows that were wanted. However, his colors were considered gaudy and too bright by some churchmen. His pictorial windows were in great demand, but many critics believed that he was at his best in abstract designs. Other critics admired his marvelous mastery of technique, but not his designs.

It was his pictorial work that made Tiffany so fashionable in America. His stained-glass windows could be seen in such prestigious institutions as the Smithsonian and Yale University. He was also responsible for ornamental windows and panels on the ferry boats that plied the Hudson River between New Jersey and Manhattan. In every state and town, everyone wanted Tiffany glass. The new class of industrial magnates commissioned him: in Pittsburgh, Andrew Carnegie; in New York, Henry Osborne Havemeyer, and Arthur Heckscher. One of Tiffany's most important patrons was the entrepreneur Joseph Raphael Delemar, who commissioned five Tiffany windows, including *The Bathers*, a fine pair of bird panels, and spherical Tiffany butterfly lampshades for his subterranean swimming-pool illumination. Five windows were commissioned by the Temple of the Latter Day Saints in Salt Lake City.

Tiffany windows were, however, expensive. Some artists began to say that Tiffany had sold out to commerce, but he claimed that he was the first American artist to design for the industrial age. He had a vision of an art industry, a museum without walls. With his success so great in America, it must have been a shock for Tiffany, on a visit to Paris in 1889 for the Exposition Universelle, to find that a window by his rival John La Farge was winning all the attention and praise for its unique color and technique. Edward Moore

Above: Detail from a window by Tiffany, The Young David as a Shepherd Boy, at St. Cuthbert's church, Edinburgh, Scotland.

Right: A Tiffany landscape window, c. 1900. Dramatic pieces like this replaced the mundane world outside with a magical world of color and light.

was also in Paris so, through him, Tiffany renewed his acquaintance with Samuel Bing and arranged that he would make windows for display in Bing's influential shop.

THE FOUR SEASONS
Their reunion resulted in a long and advantageous association, and it began with a window, *The Four Seasons*, exhibited in Paris in 1892 and later in London. It was a

"domestic" window, its descriptive panels of the four seasons enclosed by an ornamental border. The four abstract paintings of the seasons symbolically evoked the times of year with colorful vegetation and landscape, and were edged by free-flowing decorative borders with jewel-like insects of colored glass. With *The Four Seasons* Tiffany achieved the aims he had been working toward for a decade, and amazed those of his critics who had been denigrating his popular pictorial work in stained glass.

As a result of his association with Bing, a link was established between Tiffany and the French painters who seemed to be working along the same lines. Ten windows of Tiffany glass with designs by French artists chosen by Bing were commissioned: Paul Ranson designed two; Pierre Bonnard, Eugene Grasset, Henri Ibels, Ker-Xavier Roussel, Paul Serusier, Henri de Toulouse-Lautrec, Edouard Vuillard and Felix Valloton each designed one. Samuel Bing also made a survey of American art and architecture for the French government and was entertained by Tiffany on his visit.

AN ARTISTIC CREDO

The exchange of ideas encouraged both of them to increase their efforts to promote a new kind of art, to make available to a wider public objects that were both useful and beautiful, objects that could be produced for the many, not just the few. They both agreed with William Morris on the importance of keeping handicrafts alive, but Tiffany believed that materials made by machine could achieve beauty in

Left: "Summer," a panel of Louis Tiffany's The Four Seasons *window, exhibited in Paris in 1892. The window amazed his critics and established his reputation.*

the home for the masses. They were both businessmen and, as a result of their discussions, they developed greater confidence in themselves as educators of public taste.

It was Bing who inspired Tiffany to design a chapel for the World's Columbian Exhibition in Chicago in 1893. His exhibit, consisting of a chapel, a light room, and a dark room, was not ready for the opening of the fair but was shown in New York and later shipped to Chicago, where it became the sensation of the exhibition. The chapel was opulent and vibrant with luminous color. The altar was white, with a white and iridescent glass mosaic front. Behind it, the reredos was composed of a pictorial, iridescent glass mosaic, with a design of peacocks and vine scrolls, set into black marble.

TIFFANY'S CHAPEL

The mosaic was the focal point, and surmounting it was a series of concentric Romanesque round arches, decorated with relief interlaces overlaid in gold. These arches were supported by clusters of columns with carved capitals, the shafts covered with glass mosaics of reds, greens, and browns in random patterns, with pearls and semiprecious stones. Light was admitted by a series of 12 stained-glass windows and an elaborate, cruciform, bejeweled sanctuary lamp was suspended in the center of the domelike space. Flanking the chapel were the dark room in blue-green and the light room in silver and pearl, lit by a chandelier of mother of pearl.

Tiffany's chapel became a symbol of

Right: A pond-lily lamp with 12 lights of iridescent glass and a sculptured, lily-pad base. Tiffany's art brought romantic beauty to the new invention of electric lighting.

American design, but some people considered the sumptuous wealth of Tiffany Byzantine too heavy, somewhat cloying and oversweet. To European eyes, much of Tiffany's work was puzzling in its eclecticism. The problem would seem to be that Americans were looking for a truly American style that would go to form a national style. In 1897, writing in *The Studio*, Cecilia Waern made this point: "Perhaps it is one of the real achievements of L. C. Tiffany that he has caught this, given it a voice. A Tiffany room is a thing apart, with an unmistakeable American note – in spite of its eclecticism."

Left: Tiffany's apple-blossom lamp. Multicolored glass makes the shade of blossoms, with a bronze stem the trunk and spreading roots the base of the apple tree.

Below: Tiffany's Byzantine chapel. At the World's Columbian Exposition in Chicago in 1893 Americans were proud to see the progress their country had made in arts and crafts.

FAVRILE GLASS AND MASS PRODUCTION

The Paris Exposition of 1889 had far-reaching effects for Tiffany. He saw there for the first time the glass vases made by Emile Gallé of Nancy. Enameled, engraved, and tinted, they were creating a sensation for their technical brilliance and artistic merit.

Preceding page: A miniature lamp by Emile Gallé of double overlay glass and bronze. Gallé's work caused a sensation at the Paris Exposition of 1889, and had a seminal effect on Tiffany's oeuvre.

Left: The celebrated cameo vases of Emile Gallé were introduced at the Paris Exposition of 1889. Like Tiffany, Gallé drew inspiration from nature for form and decoration.

Louis Tiffany and Emile Gallé were contemporaries, and there were many resemblances between the two men. Gallé was born in 1846, two years before Tiffany. His father ran a successful decorative glassware and faience business, which he took over and built up from a small local concern to perhaps the largest luxury glassware factory in Europe. All through his career, Gallé conducted experiments and produced creations that were acclaimed. He wrote extensively about the theories that lay behind his work. He had realized that decorative glass had great scope, that glass was an infinitely variable medium. Where the Venetians and great glassmakers had been striving for crystal-clear glass and achieving brilliant effects with etching and engraving, he was producing with remarkable success colored glass with the variations and intensity of precious stones.

Gallé was an artist and an entrepreneur, talented in both spheres. Like Tiffany, he drew inspiration from nature for form and decoration, and felt the urge to achieve something new in art. Both succeeded, and reached the high point in their respective careers at the time of the triumph of Art Nouveau at the 1900 Paris Exposition. Gallé's cameo glass was already being highly praised at the 1889 exhibition and this ensured the commercial success of his Nancy factory. It made a deep impression on Tiffany, and he returned to America inspired with new challenges and fresh determination.

Other Europeans were also experimenting with glass: crackled glass was being created by Leveille; hardstone effects were being achieved by Loetz; early iridescent glass vessels were being produced by Lobmeyer, Pantin and Webb; and formal, cameo-carved vessels were being produced by various English Stourbridge, Worcestershire, firms. Arthur J. Nash, trained at Stourbridge, was the manager of one of the Webb glassworks. He was touring the United States in 1892 to promote his firm's wares when Tiffany persuaded him to join in the founding of a new glassworks and factory at Corona, Long Island.

THE CORONA WORKS

Tiffany had found that to get the glass he wanted it was essential to have his own glassworks to control chemical experiments and glass production, and he employed Nash as his chief designer and manager. Nash was a technical expert, familiar with traditional methods and modern English glassmaking techniques, and it seems certain that Tiffany could not have achieved his dramatic success without him. Nash stayed with Tiffany for 15 years, bringing his sons into the business, and they later claimed that their father had not been given due credit for his part in Tiffany's success. Certainly to Nash should go much of the praise for the superior quality of Tiffany blown glass that was maintained over the years. It is thought most likely that Nash – known as "a wizard with the blow pipe" – produced the earliest flower-form vases in free-flowing shapes.

A PHOENIX ARISES FROM THE ASHES

Soon after it opened, the Corona factory burned down. Undaunted, Tiffany rebuilt and Nash remained. The firm quickly expanded, with more glassworkers being recruited from England, and a special works within the factory being built to produce blown-glass objects. The success of the Tiffany Glass and Decorating Company, and the beauty that Tiffany blown glass achieved, came about because Nash headed a team of highly skilled craftsmen; Tiffany provided the direction, purpose, and inspiration; and he and his father, Charles Tiffany, financed the operation.

FAVRILE GLASS

In 1894 Tiffany registered Favrile as a trademark. The name derived from the Old English "fabrile," meaning handmade or belonging to a craftsman. Favrile glass, as Tiffany described

Left: A selection of Tiffany's iridescent gold vases, with Egyptian-inspired decorative motifs, dating from around 1910.

it in his autobiography, "is distinguished by certain remarkable shapes and brilliant or deeply toned colors, usually iridescent like the wings of certain American butterflies, the necks of pigeons and peacocks, the wing-covers of various beetles."

The earliest recorded glass was Egyptian, dating from around 1450 B.C. Then, colored glass was achieved with softened canes or rods of glass wound round a core into the shape of a vase. The treacly mass was then reheated to fuse the canes of colored glass together to produce wavy patterns. Glass-blowing was devised in Syria in the first century B.C. Roman glass was an offshoot of earlier Syrian and Alexandrian work, and factories were established for mass-quantity production. In Imperial Rome, glass was used as decoration in bathrooms, for wall tiles and mosaics, as well as vessels. It was this sort of glass, unearthed by archeologists, that had inspired Tiffany with its soft iridescence and that he was now trying to emulate. It called for chemical knowledge and great perseverance.

EXPERIMENTS IN FAVRILE
Tiffany's team at the Corona glassworks was soon producing an extraordinary range of lustered effects, and much of the first successful glass-blowing production was sent to Bing in Paris, who was amazed and delighted by it. By the Favrile method, all kinds of ornamental ideas could be fused into the glass: flowers floated within it magically. In some showpiece Fabrile bowls miraculous effects were produced: goldfish floating amid seaweed and clear water, all in the glass itself. The most complex were the vases in what is described as paperweight glass, so technically difficult to produce that they baffle modern glassmakers even today. Sometimes colored abstractions were produced in glass that it was impossible to repeat and these became known as accidentals.

REACTIVE PAPERWEIGHT GLASS
These are among the most rare of Tiffany vases because they were so difficult and costly to make. Reactive paperweight glass was another

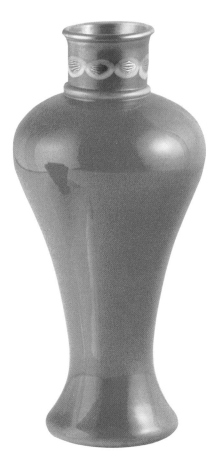

Above: Tiffany designed this Samian red vase with Egyptian designs on the neck in tribute to the craft of ancient Samos.

Left: Ttwo Tiffany intaglio vases (left), a Cypriote iridescent vase (center), and a green table center piece (right).

Far left: A virtuoso showpiece, with lifelike goldfish apparently swimming through the waterweed.

Left: Favrile paperweight vases are rare and costly. They were made by encasing a richly decorated layer of glass in a smooth outer layer so that the decoration of flowers appears trapped in the glass itself. The name itself refers to the use of a similar technique in the manufacture of French paperweights.

variation, using an inner layer of reactive glass which changed color when heated.

The millefiori method, in which little petals, flowers, or leaves were annealed all about with clear glass until a vase was formed in which the flowers hung suspended, was first developed by the Venetians in the second century B.C. Thin rods of colored glass were arranged in groups so that five white rods

grouped around a yellow rod could be cut to appear as a daisy. Supreme examples of Tiffany millefiori vases are the range of morning-glory designs. Many of these were produced later, into the twentieth century, as the technique was developed. Agate wares were produced that imitated such stones as chalcedony, jasper, agate, and marble. These effects were achieved by putting a number of variously col-

ored opaque pieces of glass into the same melting pot and heating them together.

Tiffany had filed a patent for lusterware back in 1880, describing it as "a highly iridescent one and of pleasing metallic luster changeable from one to the other, depending on the direction of the visual ray and the brilliancy or dullness of the light falling upon or passing through the glass." Luster glass was made

Above: An Agate vase (center), made c. 1910, with two marblized vases. The glass imitates the striations and veinings found in natural agate and marble.

Right: An iridescent blue Egyptian onion-flower-form vase (center), with two blue millefiori vases. These beautiful blue vases are now much sought after since fewer were produced than the more popular gold.

by dissolving salts of rare metals in the molten glass and keeping them in an oxidized state while subjecting the glass to the flame to produce the chemical reaction. Then the piece was sprayed with chloride, which made it crackle and break up into a mass of fine lines that picked up the light. Different effects were produced with different metals – pearly sheens, golden lusters, rich, deep blues. Gold luster, it was said, was formed from $20 gold pieces, and gold was also used to achieve the much sought-after red pieces.

IRIDESCENT GLASS

He did not claim to have invented iridescent glass, but Tiffany's iridescent glass had a soft, incandescent sheen, unlike the hard, mirror-

like surface of that produced by Lobmeyer and others. Many copied him, but it was said that their colors were thin and flat when compared with Tiffany pieces. Peacock-feather patterns were produced in iridescent glass, probably invented by Arthur Nash and directly inspired by Whistler's Peacock Room in London and peacocks were a recurring motif

of the Art Nouveau movement. Jack-in-the-pulpit vases, taking their name from the flower of the convolvulus, were also made in iridescent gold or blue glass. They were one of several examples of Tiffany taking a humble hedgerow flower and giving it an amazing sophistication in iridescent glass. These vases are spectacularly shaped, with single, delicate

Above: An elegant Tiffany punch bowl of iridescent gold made from nonleaded glass.

Right: A jack-in-the-pulpit vase – one of Tiffany's most successful Art Nouveau designs. The slenderness of the stem accentuates the curly corolla.

flowers poised on slender stems.

Basalt or talc was added to the molten glass to form Lava glasses. They simulated the effects of volcanic forces on glass, in a free-form kind of expressionism representing the violence of nature, in black and rough textures. In Cypriote glass, Tiffany set out to recapture the appearance of antique glass with finely pitted, nacreous surfaces, corroded and decayed by time, irregularly and abstractly patterned. This was done by rolling the glass in pulverised crumbs and then lustering the encrusted surface. Cameo glass was produced, and some particularly beautiful effects were achieved in water-lily vases overlaid in low relief. The basis for the technique of cameo-carving is a vessel of two differently colored glasses, sometimes with a layer between. A translucent yellow could be overlaid with red glass on which the outer layer was cut, carved, and ground away to leave the design in relief on the background. Tiffany used rather sickly combinations of colors at times.

THE INTRODUCTION OF FAVRILE

Although the first Favrile art glass was produced at the Corona factory in 1894, Tiffany did not launch his new product on the market for another two years. He first sent glass to Bing, and then sent examples to museums and art galleries in Europe, America, and the Far East. Tiffany's method of introducing his art glass to a worldwide, discerning audience was inspired publicity for the commercial launch of his bowls and vases and ensured an immediately favorable reception.

FROM NEW YORK TO ACCRINGTON

Joseph Briggs, another Englishman, joined Tiffany in 1890. His rise to the top of the organization was swift, and he became Tiffany's personal assistant, making a particular study of mosaic work. By 1902 he was manager of the Mosaic Department, in charge of some of the most spectacular work produced. He ran the furnaces until they closed in 1928. He sent a quantity of Tiffany glass to his family in Accrington, Lancashire and this collection, later donated to the Haworth Art Gallery in Accrington, is now the finest single collection of Tiffany glass in Europe.

GLASS ARTIFACTS

While Tiffany was developing Favrile glass and experimenting with all kinds of colored glass, much pot-metal glass of glorious color was produced which could never find a place

in the stained-glass windows. Stores of it soon accumulated and Tiffany himself said "It was evident that an industry pushed so far ought to strive to lower the annual deficit by the utilization of by-products, just like any other." This was the sound commercial reason for turning to small glass – and to lamps in particular – thus making use of the glass left over

Above: A Lava glass vase dating from 1909. In this technique, molten glass was spilled over a rough surface to produce a dramatically volcanic effect.

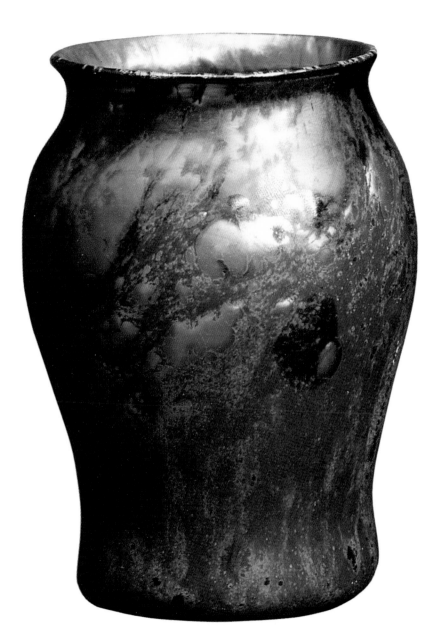

from stained-glass windows, adapting the same technique with leading. But whereas in stained glass Tiffany had had to contend against the tradition in favor of British glass and a certain timidity about the reaction to his bright colors, the success of his small glass and his lamps was immediate. They appealed to everybody and there was universal approval of their decorative charm and of the leaded shades that gave a pleasing, diffused quality to the light.

TIFFANY LAMPS

All Tiffany's favorite nature themes appear in his lamps: peacocks and dragonflies, trees in blossom, trailing flowers, and brilliant blooms. The shades were worked with a detailed juxtaposition of glass: the stems like trunks of trees and stems of flowers, the bases like roots, or like lily pads, each combining with the other to make a satisfying whole. Glass had long been employed to protect the flickering flames of oil lamps and gas. Now, with the coming of electricity, the light was stronger and harder. Tiffany lamps came at the right moment to cast a magic glow over the new, harsh, modern light that was so efficient and yet so unromantic. The commercial aspect of Tiffany's work reached its peak with the lamps, which seized the public imagination. Soon no home was complete without a Tiffany lamp, for they created interiors full of warmth and diffused light.

There were floor, ceiling, and table lamps, chandeliers, filigree lamps, spider's webs and

Left: A Cypriote vase. With Cypriote glass Tiffany set out to produce the appearence of ancient glass that had been buried for centuries: the surface corroded, pitted, and nacreous, the color and pattern haphazard.

purple globes, trellis lamps on which grapes or clematis trailed. One of the most popular was the wistaria lamp.

Many of these lamps in floral designs were the design work of the team that Tiffany had gathered around him. Whereas the Favrile vases and bowls were individually crafted, the lamps which first appeared in 1895 were so popular and the demand so great that he had so find some means of mass production. He set up an assembly line at the Corona works to put the lamps together. Hundreds, sometimes thousands, of each lamp design were made and sold. As with the vases, his imitators were many, but none matched Tiffany in terms of quality.

TIFFANY'S ARTISTS
Tiffany's team produced a constant flow of ideas, and while his creative energy provided the drive, his individual artists were allowed scope to choose colors and textures. The range of colors to choose from by the end of the century was truly amazing – as many as 5000 colors and varieties – and in this way each lamp, although mass produced, was still individual and unique. Some of the outstanding lamp designs were by women. The wistaria lamp, with its random-edged shade and multicolored tesserae intricately leaded, was the work of Mrs. Curtis Freschel, and won an award in 1902 at the International Exhibition of Modern Decorative Arts in Turin. Mrs. Clara Driscoll was responsible for the elegant dragonfly lampshade which won a prize at the Paris International Exposition in 1900. It is a lovely,

Left: An iridescent glass lamp with a base of bronze and reticulated jade-green glass. Reticulated glass is now a very rare form of Tiffany art glass.

Left: Lamp with an opalescent shade giving a pearly softness to the light.

Far left: Floor-standing lamp of 12-light lily design. The lily-light clusters make it one of the most highly priced lamps today.

imaginative piece of work; the insects, with their wings spread, hang head downward round the dome of the shade, forming a fringe effect. Each wing is made up of minute fragments of colored glass, in delicate leading, and the dome of the lamp, randomly decorated with raindrops, is set with semiprecious stones, all on a bronze, twisted vine base.

Tiffany was paying particular attention as time went on to the base of the lamps, realizing the scope that they offered for his work.

He opened a foundry and metal shop at the Corona factory in 1897 so that bronze and copper could be made on the premises. He designed the famous lily-pad lamp in bronze, with slender clusters of flower shapes springing on slender bronze stems from a lily-pad base, and it won a Grand Prize at the Turin Exhibition in 1902. The nautilus lamp design is also credited to Tiffany, the leaded glass shade emulating the convoluted nautilus shape, which contained the light fitting and the bulb. His feeling for sculptural form found expression in bronze, molded to support or hold the shades.

For the first time, Tiffany had produced items that were both useful and practical. Now the use of Favrile glass spread from flower vases and lamps to plaques, table decorations, cologne bottles, cups, plates, and tobacco jars. He extended the range to enamels and paste, bronzes and mother of pearl for jewelry boxes, cigarette cases, pin cushions, bonbon dishes, vanity, snuff and cigarette boxes, toilet boxes, and trays. His taste found expression in a thousand articles of applied art; these, occupying a prominent place in households, exercised a happy influence on the taste of citizens according to Tiffany's creed. The vases and bowls made before 1896

Above: Dragonflies with wings spread form the border of this floor lamp – one of the most popular designs produced in many variations.

Right: The wistaria table item, no. 342 in the original catalog at $350, is now one of the most highly prized Tiffany lamps.

were not meant for sale, and are therefore not signed and numbered. All the early pieces are distinctive, rare, and highly prized today. Once Favrile was launched on the market, a numbering system was instituted. This system should make it possible to date Tiffany pieces accurately, but the numbering has yet to be fully deciphered.

Samuel Bing exhibited Tiffany's Favrile glass at his new shop in Paris, La Maison de l'Art Nouveau. The shop's grand opening in 1895 was the first representative exhibition of Art Nouveau, and the 10 Tiffany windows that Bing had commissioned were displayed, as well as some 20 examples of Tiffany's blown-glass work.

A LEADING LIGHT IN ART NOUVEAU

Tiffany was to be known from then onward as the foremost American representative of Art Nouveau. Art Nouveau had emerged in its various forms, now voluptuous and exuberant, now spare and angular. The lines were different and exciting: sensuous and flowing lines; lines that bent and curved and turned and did not conform, like women's flowing hair, twisting smoke, and trailing leaves.

Art Nouveau produced different forms in different countries. It was sophisticated in France, with Lalique, who began his career designing jewelry. He was hailed as a revolutionary because of his use of nonprecious materials such as glass, and his creative designs. He moved on from jewelry to enamels and to glass. His most characteristic glass was milky-blue opalescent, colorless, and frosted, without internal decoration. His gift was in the poetic imagery of form in glass: nymphs

curve their backs, maidens cavort, doves close their wings. Lalique was luckily able to simplify his technique to reach a wide public, and there was a vast range of household glassware produced by the Lalique factory in much the same way as Tiffany glass. Lalique was a household name that endured and was continued by his family.

TIFFANY'S TRIUMPH

From 1898 Tiffany took his place on the center stage of the Art Nouveau scene and his true genius emerged at this point, free of overrich and gaudy color, free of representational figures. There was something of abstract expressionist art in Tiffany's Favrile glass that was ahead of its time.

Overriding everything was Tiffany's love of color and the shimmering changes of color fused with light – rich, opulent, and glowing. He believed that color is to the eye as music to the ears, for, as Oscar Wilde said, music is the only art that is truly nonrepresentational, and Tiffany came nearest to it with color. The spiritual strength of Tiffany's color, allied to movement and form, is at its best in the vases made before 1900. There the color harmonizes with the line, is subtle and delicate when he chooses, just as it is boldly glorious to suit other forms.

His superiority as a colorist can clearly be seen when comparing his work with that of those who copied him, for example Johannes Loetz Witwe of Klostermuhle in Austria, or Frederick Carder at the Steuben Glassworks in Corning, whom Tiffany was forced to sue in 1913.

Left: A lily lamp, a Favrile vase, and a nautilus-shell desk lamp, the shell containing the light fitting and bulb.

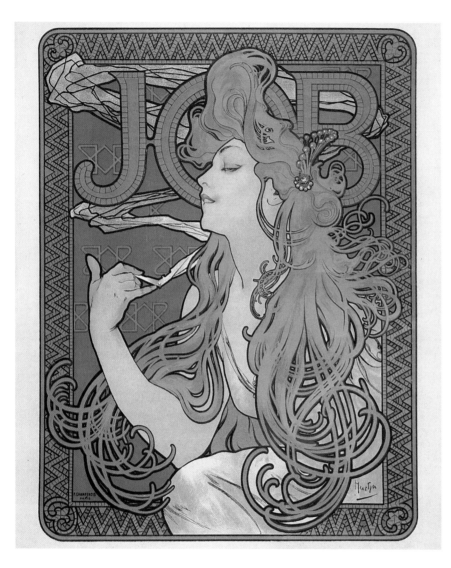

Above: Alphonse Mucha's advertisement for Job cigarettes, c. *1900. His images of languorous women made Mucha one of the first exponents of Art Nouveau in Paris.*

The immense popularity of Tiffany's Favrile glass, and the day-to-day business of his organization left little time for interior-design projects, but some major schemes demanded his personal attention, and in these he was to develop further his interest in mosaic. Tiffany mosaics were designed on walls, like paintings. Many were produced over a period of 40 years, and were remarkable in their size and scope. There was a mosaic for the Catholic cathedral of St. Louis, Missouri, to a design by the Italian artist Aristide Leonari, which spread over 27,870 square meters (300,000 square feet). Mosaics were used in the chapel designed for the 1893 World Fair in Chicago, which created a sensation with its Byzantine richness. Mosaic featured specially in the Fifth Avenue home of millionaire Henry O. Havemeyer, where Tiffany surprised his critics again with a fresh, unexpected creative approach. The eclectic mixture of ornaments, hanging lamps, Oriental and Islamic splendor was restrained now, for he now had a more mature grasp of harmonies. There were sensational features – the hanging staircase, the white mosaic hall, the library ceiling hung with a mosaic of multicolored silk, the pillared entrance, the Japanese lacquers – but they were a unified whole.

Tiffany followed this success with another major project, the design and installation of a memorial window for the new library at Yale University. The 9 x 1.5m (30 x 5ft) window was donated by Samuel B. Chittendon in memory of his daughter, Mary Lusk, and Tiffany incorporated 20 figures into the design, linking them in a repetitive decorative motif.

THE MEXICAN MOSAIC

The colossal glass drop-curtain at the National Theater in the Palace of Fine Arts in Mexico

Right: Lalique's Suzanne au Bain, c. 1925. Lalique's brilliance in glassmaking was different to Tiffany's, in that he was not so concerned with color or internal decoration.

Far right: An unusual Tiffany floor lamp of entwined and twisted stems with a flower-headed light. The essentially Art Nouveau styling of this lamp still has a modern look nearly a hundred years later.

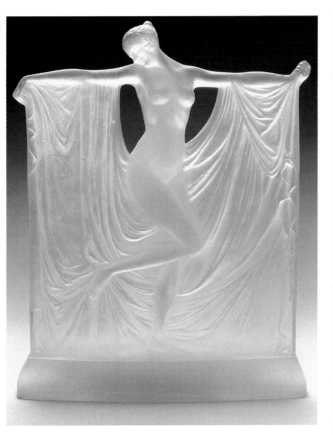

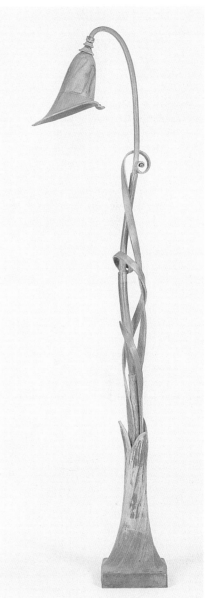

City demonstrated the sheer splendor of Tiffany's work in mosaic. This commission involved a model produced by the painter and stage designer Harry Stoner, a landscape panorama of the view from the presidential palace with snow-capped mountain peaks. It was translated by Tiffany's team at the Corona factory into a glass mosaic of 167 square meters (1800 square feet) containing almost a million tesserae and weighing some 27 tons. It went on display in New York before being shipped to Mexico City, where it was built into a finely engineered construction that took only seconds to raise and lower. Audiences in Mexico were given a luxury of applied art unknown to opera- and theater-goers in London, Paris, and New York. The fire curtain was a thick wall separating stage from auditorium. It was like a vast window, square-mullioned with a landscape beyond of flowers, lakes, pastures, hills, a mountain range, volcanoes, and the snowy caps of Popocatépetl and Ixtaccihuatl, with the lovely clouds of sunset shimmering beyond. The color was wrought in mosaic, and the illusion was helped by illumination.

THE CURTIS COMMISSION

The immediate result for Tiffany was a commission for a mosaic for the Curtis Publishing Company – a glass vista for its new building in Philadelphia. The building was almost complete, but there was no mural for the large place which clearly demanded one. Edward Bok, editor of *Ladies' Home Journal,* had commissioned three artists to make a design for the mural, but each had died before producing a sketch. He organized a competition of muralists, but rejected all their offerings.

THE DREAM GARDEN

Finally he recalled Maxfield Parrish, the artist, telling him of a dream garden that he would like to construct at his summer house, and introduced him to Tiffany, "with the result that the two became enthusiastic to cooperate in trying the experiment."

When completed, the mosaic was 15 meters long and 4.6 meters high (49 feet long and 15 feet high). *The Dream Garden* would be applauded for many years to come.

Right: Detail of The Dream Garden *glass mosaic made in 1915 for the Curtis Publishing Company after a design by Maxfield Parrish.*

TIFFANY'S DECLINE AND REHABILITATION

The turn of the century was the time when Tiffany brought his art glass to its highest peak of creative brilliance. The 1900 Paris Exposition was a triumph for him and for Art Nouveau. Tiffany father and son were showered with honors: Louis was created a Chevalier de la Légion d'Honneur and won a coveted gold medal; his father's firm, Tiffany & Co., won three *grand prix*, ten gold, ten silver, and two bronze medals. Clara Driscoll won a prize for the dragonfly Tiffany lamp. Louis Tiffany was then 52, and he was world famous.

As president of the Tiffany Glass and Decorating Company, he was artistic director of over a hundred skilled workers. He could design and experiment and still keep tight control of work at the studios and at the Corona factory. He was regarded as a good employer. He was evidently a perfectionist, but he was willing and able to show how perfection could be achieved, and he was generous with

Left: The lotus lamp of leaded glass with a bronze base has delicately colored shade with a Far Eastern shape.

Preceding page: The poinsettia lamp – the appeal of Tiffany lamps was immediate, the public demand enormous.

praise and encouragement, as well as criticism. He was remarkable in giving opportunities to women at that time, training women workers, encouraging them to try their skills and take an active part in the business.

In 1901 he was chosen as decorator for the Yale Bicentennial. His decoration of orange Japanese lanterns, blue flags, and evergreens in the campus was very effective, and Yale showed its appreciation by awarding Tiffany an honorary degree. His artistic achievements were marked with more awards into the new century in Europe and America, as well as ever-increasing sales. This was the Tiffany art industry in full swing, and the rate of production was prodigious.

RETAIL METHODS

Prices were high – $750, for example, for one of the lamps – and Tiffany's methods of retailing were unusual in that he set the prices on a strictly sale-or-return basis; the glass remained his property. He did not sell to shops and stores: he supplied the glass for them to sell, the retailer taking commission on the sale. If the glass was unsold after three months, it was returned to the factory; if it failed to be sold by three different retailers, it would be given away, discounted, or often destroyed.

As sales continued to increase, the Corona factory expanded to become Tiffany Furnaces. The Tiffany Glass and Decorating Company became Tiffany Studios. Arthur Nash was now assisted by his two sons, Douglas and Leslie, and Dr. Parker McIllhiney led a team of research chemists.

ORIENTAL LINES

Tiffany Furnaces was devoted to the production of glass and glass objects, while Tiffany Studios began to expand after 1900 into all the various sectors of interior decoration and household objects. The decorating service of Tiffany Studios carried a full line of Oriental rugs and fabrics for upholstery and drapes in patterns that were designed to harmonize with Tiffany glassware.

An enameling company was set up and Tiffany provided sketches for enamelwork to be carried out by a small unit, with Julia Munsen in charge, using models from his great collection of Oriental and Islamic *objets d'art*, Chinese cloisonné and Japanese sword guards. Enamels were exhibited at the Buffalo, New York, Exhibition of 1901 and were much admired for their astonishing range of colors, from translucent to opaque. Another range of vitreous enamel work was undertaken, ground glass being applied to metal objects and fired in the furnace until the glass fused to the metal to create a shimmering, iridescent effect. The

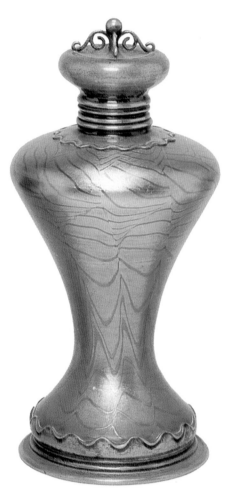

Above: Tiffany's objets d'art fused his beautiful, iridescent glass with elegant shapes and decorative motifs in metal.

Left: A circular enameled copper wall plaque with a decoration of nasturtiums.

metal objects were made in the Corona foundry in copper, brass, or bronze, and ranged from small vases to ornamental boxes to lamp bases.

After 1900 Tiffany Studios produced desk sets in glass and bronze and enamel inlaid with glass or mother of pearl in many different patterns; ashtrays, tableware, ceramic lamp bases, cigarette boxes, and lighters, inkstands, jardinières, clocks, photograph frames, pin cushions, decanters, cologne bottles, goblets, plates, plaques, and dishes. Some pottery pieces were made, but the pottery produced could not match the beauty of the glass and was discontinued. Favrile-glass dinner services were very popular and became fashionable as wedding presents. Matched sets of 48 pieces were produced in a dozen related shapes, in gold or blue iridescent glass, sometimes engraved in a grapevine design.

TIFFANY JEWELRY

Tiffany also tried his hand at jewelry, for, as he said, "a painter born with a sense of color must revel in the deep set richness of precious gems." And, of course, he had access to the stones and gems amassed by Tiffany & Co. Some very fine pieces were produced: for example, a peacock necklace with a mosaic centerpiece of opals, amethysts, and sapphires and a pendant below of a single large ruby. At the Paris Salon of 1906 some notable Tiffany pieces were shown with a distinctly Art Nouveau form: for example, a dragonfly hatpin set with opals on platinum, dandelions, and blackberries of opals. One brooch, described as "a marine motif, half crab, half octopus with writhing feet," attracted particular praise. Tiffany's jewelry was very expensive to make as so much time was spent on it, however, and financially it was not a success. Jewelry production ceased in 1916.

On the death of his father in 1902, it became necessary for Louis to give more time and attention to the affairs of Tiffany & Co.

Below: The Tiffany art industry was in full swing in the early twentieth century and there was a great demand for everything it produced. It was always artistic and of high quality, like this jardinière.

Left: The mansion at Oyster Bay, Long Island, had a high terrace overlooking Cold Spring Harbor.

He became artistic director and vice-president, with Charles T. Cook as president. All the glassmaking departments of Tiffany Studios were then moved to an impressive building on the corner of Madison Avenue and 45th Street, where they remained until 1918. Later in the same year Tiffany purchased a property called Laurelton Hall.

LAURELTON HALL

It was an old-fashioned hotel with 580 acres at Oyster Bay, Long Island, with a long shoreline facing Cold Spring Harbor, and there Tiffany planned a new mansion for himself. The hotel was demolished and Tiffany set about designing the house, the gardens, and the interior to make it a showpiece property.

He began by modeling the landscape and the elevations in clay and wax. The layout of the steel-frame building was asymmetrical, with a stream running through the center of an enclosed court, watched over by an immense Japanese bronze dragon. Visitors were immediately impressed by the fountain, water bubbling from a glass jar in the shape of a Greek amphora which changed color in a magical way with the effect of sunlight and running water. Approached from the drive, a bell tower came into view first, with the main entrance at an upper level between columns of granite and ceramic mosaics. Blue iridescent tiles on the lintel provided a recurring color note, repeated in the domed skylight over the central court. In all there were 84 rooms and 25 bathrooms, and a high terrace overlooked Cold Spring Harbor, where there was a private yacht basin.

From the shore, the house appeared mushroom-shaped, like a mosque, rounded copper roofing the house and the tower. It was a major Art Nouveau achievement in America, quite unique, and it became the most publicized home in the United States. From the photographs of Laurelton Hall, it would appear that the synthesis of structure and form was not wholly achieved, however; the styling was somewhat heavy handed. Either side of the central court were the living room and dining room, designed as a light room and a dark room, an idea that Tiffany had introduced for the Chicago Fair chapel in 1893.

THE INTERIOR

The light room was the most successful. The dining room stretched the whole width of the house; the colors were light and fresh, clear plate-glass from floor to frieze let in the daylight, the furnishings were simple and sparse and the ornament restrained. There was a rectangular fireplace faced with green marble and a mantle with three clocks. An outdoor-indoor effect was achieved with a glass-enclosed veranda – partly clear glass, partly stained glass

Right: Tiffany displayed his stained-glass masterpieces at Laurelton Hall. The Bathers *appeared to fine effect in an alcove in the living room.*

with a wistaria design. The dimly lit living room featured Tiffany's stained glass which he had saved for display in his own home. *Feeding the Flamingoes* from the Chicago Fair; his *Four Seasons* window, cut into separate panels and set into the wall; *Flowers, Fish and Fruit,* designed in 1885; *Eggplants,* from 1880. Later he added the largest window, *The Bathers,* intended for exhibition in San Francisco but withdrawn by Tiffany because he was not satisfied with the lighting arrangements. The living room had a cavelike fireplace with a bearskin rug, and there were heavy iron lighting fixtures in turtleback style. The cornices curved into the ceiling creating an attractive effect.

A CHANGE OF LIFESTYLE

There were also rooms for his Native American collections, an octagonal Chinese room for the Oriental antiques, tea rooms, a music room, and a palm house full of exotic plants. The overall effect was theatrical and a bit overpowering, like a dream fantasy. Louise, the second Mrs. Tiffany, died before the house was finished, and Louis himself now seemed to turn to a theatrical lifestyle and became notably ever more eccentric. He sought the limelight in public, but was a tyrant at home until, by 1914, one daughter had died of tuberculosis and the remaining daughters had married. Tiffany was left very lonely in his large, magnificent mansion.

There was a new note of criticism of his work from about 1903, when an article appeared in *The Craftsman*:: "The name of Tiffany promised us an admirable display, but we must confess to have been deeply disappointed . . . We are indeed far from the exquisite specimens of Mr. Tiffany's earlier manner." It had become obvious, certainly to the cognoscenti, that the creation of unique, individual, objects had been reduced. The production of matched sets of place settings, desk sets, lamps and lighting fixtures, vases and bowls in fine materials and popular designs was sufficient, at least in Tiffany's view, to maintain his position as the world's foremost industrial artist.

A NEW DIRECTION

He was the victim of his own success and he was doing too much. More and more he was having to rely on other designers to come up with ideas for the glassmakers, for his output was in great demand. But he was losing some of his most talented staff as they left and set up in competition. He was still winning awards and prizes at American exhibitions, but he wanted more than this. He never doubted his own values, but he was becoming impatient with the inability of the American critics and populace to grasp his concepts of beauty. He decided to make himself better known as an arbiter of taste and upholder of artistic values, with an entertainment and lavish spectacle that would long be remembered as an esthetic experience of the most superior kind: an Egyptian fête in New York at which the splendor of Ancient Egypt was recreated under the direction of Joseph Lindon Smith. But it was the social columnists who raved over the party, not the art critics.

At the same time there were reports of the Armory Show exhibition, where the American public saw for the first time the works of Matisse, the Fauves, the Cubists, and the German Expressionists. Here were artists who were deliberately turning the human figure into geometric cubes, expressing every movement with angular lines and sharp, spare images – and being praised for it. It was a highly significant and sensational art exhibition. Tiffany was shocked and confused by it, seeing in its ugliness a rejection of all his own values. He was disconcerted to find that many leading American artists were included, yet

Right: A sophisticated bronze and glass filigree table lamp whose metal base perfectly complements the shade.

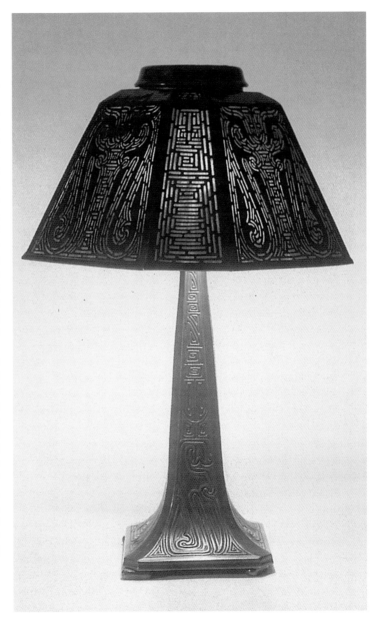

he himself had not been asked to participate. Feeling threatened, he spoke out against "these modernists," unaware that the shock he had received from their work was comparable with the sensation he himself had created with his unorthodox treatment of color, glass, and form in his day.

TIFFANY IN DECLINE

He could not accept that his day was over. As he felt the tide of fashion turning against him, his own reaction became more extreme, such as in the staging of his birthday masque, *The Quest of Beauty*, in 1916. He also decided to record his achievements in a memorial volume published at his own expense: *The Art Work of Louis C. Tiffany*. The text of the book consists of a series of interviews in which Tiffany dictated his views to Charles de Kay, under headings he himself chose. The book was never sold: only three hundred copies were distributed to those whom Tiffany considered deserving recipients.

He had been fortunate in his timing at many points in his career, but now the times were against him. The harsh realities of World War I had produced a general postwar reaction to the flamboyant extravagances and the gilded artifacts of the turn of the century, which were seen as decadent. The world had become more austere. The richly gilded, colorful stained glass of Tiffany's heyday was being rejected on all sides. Tiffany was, in fact, an apt example of what had happened to Art Nouveau, in that the 1900 Exhibition was at once the climax

Left: The magnolia vase created for the World's Columbia Exposition of 1893. It was made when America wanted decorative opulence and magnificence, but is now too ornate and elaborate for modern taste.

and the finale of it. Once it became popular and available to a wider public and had to be produced in large quantities, its vigor and exuberance were diluted and a deterioration of design set in. As cheapened versions of the originals were produced, the very vulgarization that Art Nouveau had been created to combat overtook Art Nouveau itself and the boldest designers began to experiment in new directions, while many influential figures retired from the scene.

THE TIFFANY FOUNDATION

Tiffany began to work out a plan for a school of rational art in America with a museum attached: "a place where are gathered examples of art decoration from various periods and countries." This special museum school became a reality in 1918, when the Louis Comfort Tiffany Foundation was set up with a substantial endowment for art education and Laurelton Hall provided as a retreat for students and artists. Nineteen approved students began their nonacademic art education based on Tiffany's principle of art-by-absorption in 1920. A large percentage of the young men and women who became resident members at Laurelton Hall continued in art, craft, and design careers, including Hugh McKean, who later said: "We had nothing to do all day except work where and how we wished on our art . . . Mr. Tiffany seemed to be pleased at the happiness he was giving us."

Tiffany continued to oversee various projects and his last major commission was the decoration of the Presidential Palace in Havana, Cuba. The furnishings were mainly period reproductions, but included 23 Tiffany rugs and 15 Tiffany lamps. The building that housed Tiffany Studios at 345 Madison Avenue was sold at the time that the art

Above: A brilliantly colored mosaic section of iridescent glass tesserae, rescued from the Philadelphia Mint.

foundation was launched, moving to smaller showrooms in Madison Avenue and then, finally, to 46 West 23rd Street. The production of collectors' items ceased after the war. When the entire stock was offered at a clearance sale in 1920, many items in the stock had been unsold for many years.

THE CLOSURE OF TIFFANY FURNACES

Tiffany Furnaces was under the management of A. Douglas Nash from 1919, and production was soon curtailed. The market was then being flooded with Carnival glass, which was mass-produced by being pressed or molded and then dipped to give a thin coating of pale iridescence. Tiffany withdrew his financial support from Tiffany Furnaces, because of increasing commercialization, he said, and within a few months the production of Favrile glass ceased for ever. Joseph Briggs remained in charge of the retail organization, selling off the stocks still held, but in 1932 he filed a petition for bankruptcy. The firm managed to struggle on for a few more years, but it was a sad end to the high ideals of Louis Comfort Tiffany, its creator. To Briggs went the task of disposing of the stock, at various auctions, for a fraction of its cost price.

TIFFANY'S DEATH

Tiffany himself seems to have lived like a recluse during his eighties, neglected, disappointed, his work regarded as irrelevant by the art world of the day. He died on January 17, 1933, mourned by few, forgotten by many.

Right: Sulfur Crested Cockatoos, *the glass mosaic exhibition piece in the Haworth Art Gallery, Accrington, Lancashire. It is traditionally attributed to Joseph Briggs, Tiffany's right-hand man.*

Tiffany's name faded into obscurity; the beautiful things he had created were discarded. It was sad that he died when his reputation was in eclipse. The silence continued for many years after his death and the records of his achievements were destroyed.

Joseph Briggs had assembled his own collection of Tiffany art glass and in 1933, when he returned to England, he gave half his collection to his family and friends and presented the town of Accrington, Lancashire, with the rest. At the time his gift of unfashionable art glass cannot have seemed very acceptable to a town where unemployment was increasing and there was much poverty. It is strange to think of the light, bright, colorful, sophisticated Tiffany glass finding a place among the "dark satanic mills" of Lancashire – but great good fortune that it did. The collection of 120 pieces was displayed in the town museum and was later transferred to the Haworth Art Gallery, where it remained unknown to American collectors all through the years of Tiffany's obscurity. It is now the largest collection of Tiffany glass in Europe.

THE CLOSURE OF LAURELTON HALL

At Laurelton Hall the Tiffany Foundation was struggling with soaring costs. After World War II the estate was sold off and art scholarships were funded with the proceeds. The entire contents of Laurelton Hall – the treasures of a lifetime's collecting – were sold at auction in New York in 1946 at a fraction of their original value. To complete the extinction of Tiffany's glory, Laurelton Hall was

Right: Red is one of the most sought after Tiffany colors, and is rare and costly today. The color was derived from compounds of gold.

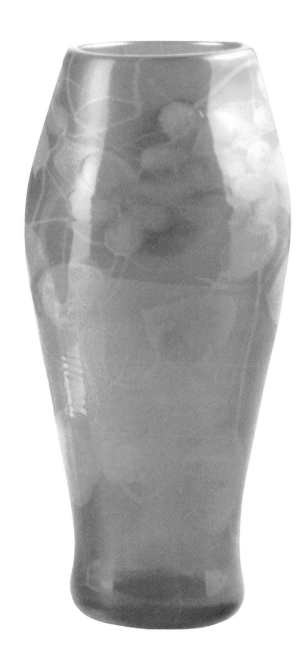

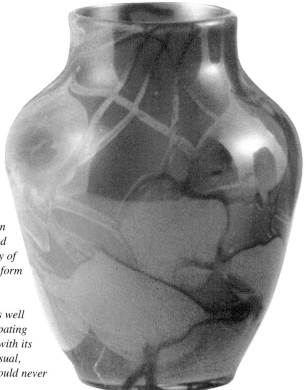

Far right: It would be an insensitive eye that failed to respond to the artistry of Tiffany's slender flower-form vases in Favrile glass.

Right: Favrile glass was well ahead of its time, anticipating abstract impressionism with its free-form design and casual, accidental effects that could never be repeated.

destroyed by fire. Its former owner's reputation began to revive from the ashes of this fire, however, 25 years after his death.

All through the 1930s and 1940s his name had been "cloaked with derision," as the Bauhaus functional and austere German style was adopted in America. Tiffany was condemned on all counts: too ornamental, too colorful, altogether too richly decorative, and at the same time too commercial. But early in the 1950s an interest in Tiffany glass began to emerge among antique dealers and museum curators. During the next decade interest in his

work continued to grow and there was a revival of interest in iridescence. The rediscovery of Tiffany coincided with the reappraisal of Art Nouveau during the 1960s; people began to discover that the work of the Art Nouveau designers looked surprisingly modern. Gradually, Tiffany glass tiles and lamps and other items were being incorporated into interior designs. Good examples of Favrile vases were on their way to becoming collector's items, valued as period antiques, their style and quality characterizing the high point of American decorative arts in the Art Nouveau style; and historians began to mark Tiffany's place as a gifted and original artist.

ACCUMULATING TIFFANY COLLECTIONS

Another major step was taken in the reestablishment of Tiffany's reputation as a pioneer of modern design when the Byzantine chapel he designed for the World Fair of 1893 was resurrected in Winter Park, Florida. The Morse Gallery of Art, now at Winter Park, has the most important collection of Tiffany material in the world today, some 4000 items. America had finally become aware of its outstanding indigenous designer and realized that he had been shamefully neglected.

ABSTRACT EXPRESSIONISM

The advent of abstract expressionism in America brought Tiffany to the attention of painters in this genre like Jackson Pollock and Robert Motherwell, who saw him as an early exponent of pure form and color in art expressed in glass form. It began to be realized that the unique quality of Tiffany was the freedom with which the glass was handled. It was seen that, without violating the character of the material itself, Tiffany and his craftsmen had produced an amazing series of blown-glass objects decorated in the highest order of good design. And Tiffany's skill in embodying accidental effects to enhance the glass and its decoration was seen as well ahead of its time.

ROCKETING SALE PRICES

The increasing interest in Tiffany art glass was

Right: The peony lamp – Tiffany's work is now highly sought after, the trend in prices ever upward, and lamps go even higher today in price than vases.

soon reflected in prices, which spiraled upward dramatically. A dragonfly lamp, for example, that had cost $125 brand new in 1928, sold for $2250 in 1967; these lamps are now highly sought after, and sell in excess of $80,000 in Christie's New York sales. The highest prices are for the large wistaria lamps with the undulating rim – in excess of $120,000 – and the lily-light clusters. There is no doubt that Tiffany would have thoroughly enjoyed the praise, the appreciation and the high prices of his work – and would have considered it the tribute due to his genius.

Looking back at his success a century later, it is clear to see how he stands out, overshadowing anything produced at that particular time by his sheer range and quality. Tiffany moved the technique of art glass into a different plane. Before his time lamps might have been designed with a decoration of wistaria; it was Tiffany who went further and created a lamp that is a tree – blossom, leaves, trunk, roots, and all.

With his reestablishment, high claims have been made for Tiffany, but there still remains today the opinion of some critics that

Below: Green and gold flowers form vases of graceful and delicate shape that are enhanced by the internal impression of leaves in the glass.

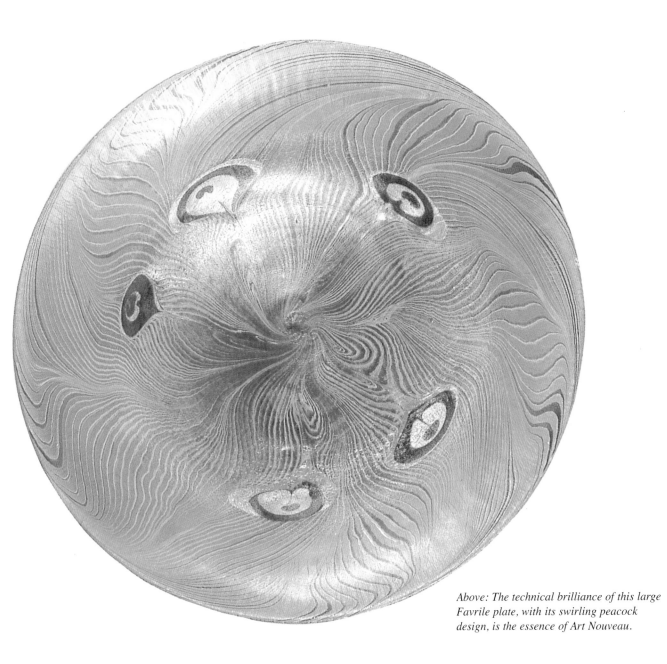

Above: The technical brilliance of this large Favrile plate, with its swirling peacock design, is the essence of Art Nouveau.

Right: Cameo vases with a theme of lilies. Tiffany's place as an artist is upheld by vases such as these.

Tiffany is more kitsch than genius, a feeling that he went too far. Certainly, some of the Tiffany Studios' production became repetitive.

But he was the first industrial artist, and the mixture of highly creative artistic and technical skills with commercial production was a new and difficult role to control. In fact, this qualification continues to make Tiffany a difficult artist to classify.

TIFFANY'S LEGACY

Tiffany had many imitators, but he was the originator. Tiffany and Gallé had an originality and genius when working in the medium of glass that few could match. It became in their hands a medium of personal statement of ideals and visions, not just a vase or a lamp.

Both men have taken and passed the test of time, and their places in decorative art are no longer subject to the swings of fashion. Today the Tiffany name remains synonymous with glamour and luxury, beauty and color, iridescence and opalescence, and the illumination of richly glowing light.

Tiffany's is a dramatic story, full of vitality and glamour, of a man convinced of his own genius, of an adventurous man who was confident enough to be unorthodox; a man with the advantages and the talent to pursue his own artistic aims and to achieve greatness; a man who has been ignored and then vindicated by time.